ART FRAUD
DETECTIVE

ANNA NILSEN

KINGFISHER

For Elaine
From ATB

KINGFISHER

Kingfisher Publications Plc
New Penderel House
283–288 High Holborn
London WC1V 7HZ

First published in 2000
This paperback edition first published in 2005
2 4 6 8 10 9 7 5 3 1

1TR/01/05/TWP/MA/150ENSOMA/F

Author and forgery artwork: Anna Nilsen
Editor: Camilla Reid
Senior Designer: Sarah Goodwin
DTP: Nicky Studdart
Production Controller: Caroline Jackson
Illustrator: Andy Parker

The Publishers would also like to thank the following:
Sinead and Rowan Derbyshire, Elaine Ward,
Erika Langmuir and Suzie Burt.

THE MYSTERY CALLER

At the Town Gallery Mr Bassett, the old security guard, receives a phone call from someone with a strange, muffled voice. It looks like the gallery may have a bit of a problem...

RING! RING!

ZZZ

Hello?

Mr Bassett? I have some very important information that could save your gallery from total disaster!

What the...! Who is this?

You silly old fool, call yourself a security guard?! Under your nose, THIRTY of your paintings have been stolen – by four notorious gangs of forgers – and replaced by cunning FAKES! If you want to catch the forgers and stop the real paintings being sold on the black market...

...you'd better find the fakes, FAST! You want to know who I am? All I can tell you is that I am a member of one of the gangs but I've had enough of life as a criminal. Out of all the forgers, I was the only one who refused to get involved in the Town Gallery job.

3

For my own safety, I'm keeping my identity secret and staying in disguise until those devious villains are locked up behind bars. However, if you're smart, you may be able to work out my identity. Oh, one last thing... each gang member, apart from me, has forged exactly TWO paintings!

...and then the line went dead.

This is a catastrophe for the Town Gallery! If we go to the experts for help, people will find out that our paintings aren't the real thing – we'll have to close down and the masterpieces will be lost forever.

But, hang on... if I had a fast-working private detective to search the gallery and find the forgeries, we could be saved. And I've got an idea! How about...

YOU?

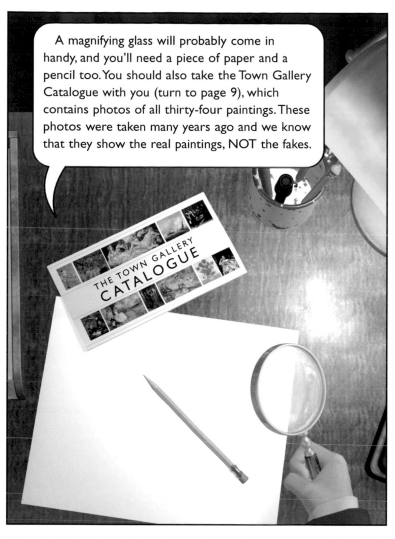

A magnifying glass will probably come in handy, and you'll need a piece of paper and a pencil too. You should also take the Town Gallery Catalogue with you (turn to page 9), which contains photos of all thirty-four paintings. These photos were taken many years ago and we know that they show the real paintings, NOT the fakes.

Now, I must confess that I've known about these forgers for a little while. This letter arrived from the police the other day but I'm afraid that I hadn't taken much notice of it up till now.

TO ART GALLERIES WORLDWIDE:
FORGER ALERT!
ISSUED BY THE
INTERNATIONAL POLICE ALLIANCE

Four gangs of art forgers are known to be operating internationally. Each gang has four members who work as a team, dividing the profits of their crimes between them. The gangs are fierce rivals and compete with each other to steal paintings from galleries around the world, replacing them with their worthless forgeries. Unfortunately not enough evidence has yet been found to convict the forgers. THEY ARE STILL ON THE LOOSE – BE ON YOUR GUARD!

The police also sent me a poster which shows the four gangs of forgers. I've pinned it to my noticeboard and you'll need to take a closer look at it. I have a feeling that it will be very useful in helping you find out which are the fake paintings, and who forged them.

Turn to the next page to see the poster close up...

ART FRAUD

ISSUED TO ART GALLERIES WORLDWIDE BY THE INTERNATIONAL POLICE ALLIANCE

Each gang of forgers is secretly proud of its work and stamps all
its fakes with one particular symbol, hidden somewhere in the painting.
The International Police Alliance has also discovered that each forger
makes a set number of deliberate, tiny changes to every painting

FISH GANG

Name: Molly Mullet
Number of changes: 1

Name: Claude Conger
Number of changes: 2

Name: Bonnie Barracuda
Number of changes: 3

Name: Attila Anchovy
Number of changes: 4

BIRD GANG

Name: Genghis Gull
Number of changes: 1

Name: Lizzie Lapwing
Number of changes: 2

Name: Hawley Hornbill
Number of changes: 3

Name: Imelda Ibis
Number of changes: 4

SUSPECTS

that he or she forges. As a kind of signature, each forger always makes exactly the same number of changes. **By locating the hidden symbol and counting the changes, it is possible to identify the forger who made each fake**. The gangs and their members are as follows:

STAR GANG

Name: Portia Pollux
Number of changes: 1

Name: Bugsy Betelgeux
Number of changes: 2

Name: Saffron Sirius
Number of changes: 3

Name: Vasile Vega
Number of changes: 4

TREE GANG

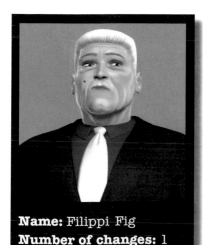

Name: Filippi Fig
Number of changes: 1

Name: Annie Apricot
Number of changes: 2

Name: Josef Juniper
Number of changes: 3

Name: Salome Spruce
Number of changes: 4

LOOK FOR THE CLUES!

It's time to start your detective work

Enter the Town Gallery on the next page. The bottom section of the book is the Town Gallery Catalogue which contains all the works of art, and is arranged alphabetically according to the surname of the artist. Let's start by looking at the first painting in the gallery. Find the matching picture in the catalogue and compare them.

If the picture is a forgery it will contain a hidden symbol and between one and four changes… I've found a tree symbol! So, this picture has been forged by a member of the Tree Gang. I can also see that the forger has added another shoe, removed the beads, and changed the colour of the woman's waistband. So there are three changes in total.

Now turn back to the Art Fraud Suspects poster. By matching the tree symbol with three changes, I can deduce that Josef Juniper forged the painting by Jan van Eyck.

On your piece of paper, draw a chart like this. Fill in the artist and the forger as you find them. If you discover a real painting, fill it into the bottom section. The mystery caller did not do any forgeries so his or her name will be missing from the chart.

Your mission is to…

1. Name the four real paintings.

2. Find out who made each fake. (Remember, every forger, except for the mystery caller, has made two fakes.)

3. Identify the mystery caller (the only name missing from your chart!)

GOOD LUCK!

If you need some help, turn to page 45.
The answers are on pages 46–47, but don't cheat!

HENDRICK **AVERCAMP** 1585–1634 **Holland**

A Winter Scene with Skaters near a Castle 1608 or 1609

Oil paint on oak panel 41 x 41 cm

Profoundly deaf, and unable to speak, Avercamp was known as 'the mute of Kampen'. He specialized in finely detailed winter scenes, filled with movement and dotted with lots of tiny figures. Although he painted cold, snowy scenes, he usually used a palette of warm colours, such as pink and brown, in his pictures.

The buildings in *A Winter Scene with Skaters near a Castle* are painted from the imagination but the skaters and tobogganers are based on watercolour drawings made from life. Returning to his studio, Avercamp would use his sketches to create his carefully composed paintings, grouping the figures, holding hands and dancing, to make patterns within the picture. In this scene, we can see that because of the freezing weather, all work – fishing, farming and brewing, for example – has stopped and everyone, rich and poor, is out having fun on the ice.

JAN VAN **EYCK**

THE TOWN GALLERY
CATALOGUE

PIERO DELLA FRANCESCA

PAOLO **UCCELLO**

RAPHAEL

JAN **GOSSAERT**

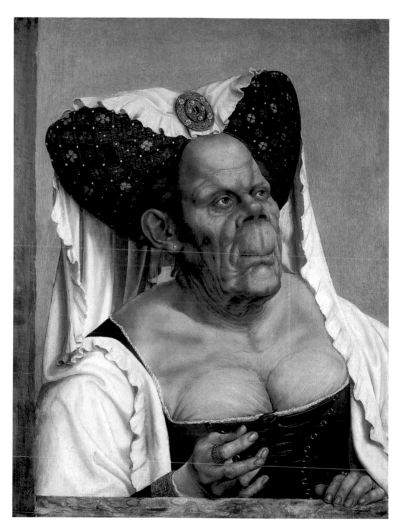

HANS **HOLBEIN**

JAN **BRUEGHEL**

HENDRICK **AVERCAMP**

WILLEM VAN DE **VELDE**

JAN **VERMEER**

THOMAS **GAINSBOROUGH**

E **WATTEAU** 1684–1721 **France**

■ 8

artist, and the first artist
'fêtes galantes' – scenes of
...selves in the open air.
...men and women, then
...e they wore extravagant
...g fun.

...s a picture about the
...ple in the foreground
...nd they lean together
... make a bridge
...gs, we can see that
...hind, a statue of a
... the background

JAN VAN OS

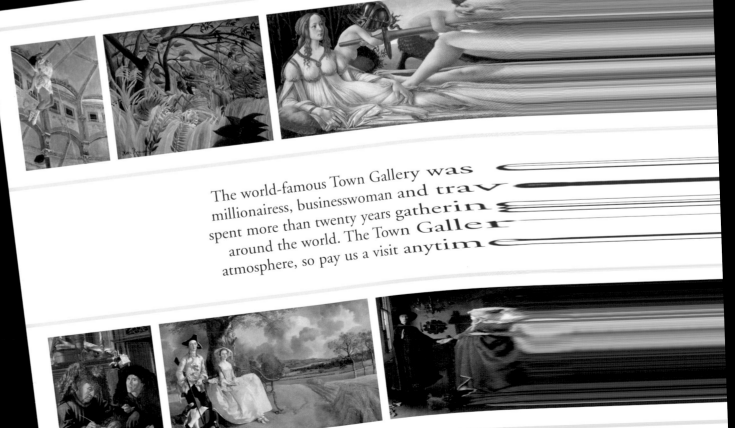

The world-famous Town Gallery was
millionairess, businesswoman and trav
spent more than twenty years gatherin
around the world. The Town Galler
atmosphere, so pay us a visit anytime